INTRO

INTRODUCTION 2
   TYPES OF ANALYSIS 3
      FUNDAMENTAL ANALYSIS 3
      TECHNICAL ANALYSIS 3
JAPANESE CANDLES 6
   CANDLE CHART TEMPORALITIES 6
   TYPES OF JAPANESE CANDLES 9
TYPES OF TREND 12
   TREND LINE 12
   TYPES OF TREND 12
   WHAT HAPPENS WHEN AN INVESTMENT FUND OR A BIG BANK ENTERS THE GAME? 14
   THE IMPORTANCE OF THE NEWS 14
   TEMPORALITIES. 15
   (MAIN, SECONDARY AND THIRD TREND) 15
      MAIN TREND 16
      SECONDARY TREND 16
      THIRD TREND 17
SUPPORTS AND RESISTANCES 18
   TECHNICAL INDICATORS 19
THE STRATEGY 22
   COMPONENTS OF THE STRATEGY 23
      MONETARY MANAGEMENT 23
      THE MULTIPLIER (LEVERAGE) 23
      RULES TO OPERATE 24
APPLYING THE STRATEGY TO THE OPERATION 24
   PERSONAL RECOMMENDATION 29

THE BEST WAY TO OPERATE THE FOREX MARKET

INTRODUCTION

In the stock markets there are different financial products where we can operate and these days it is much easier to access them. A few years ago, when the Internet was not available to the majority of the world's population, the only way to invest was through financial intermediaries who worked and still work in brokerage houses and investment banks around the world.

However, now in our time it is only necessary to have a computer with Internet access, a broker that provides us with a platform, and in less than a second we ourselves will be able to invest and make personal decisions about our financial assets. Still, despite the great technological advances we have today and the abundant information we can receive about investments in the stock markets, this does not guarantee that we can benefit from it. On the contrary, the lack of information will make us lose money and I speak from my own experience.

So if you are interested in learning how to invest in the stock markets it is important that you educate yourself first to avoid losing your money.

Various financial products exist in the stock markets or stock exchanges. It is the same as when we go to a traditional supermarket in our city, and we see that inside they have several items for sale. The concept is the same, however, the use we will give to these products is different.

For example, in the stock markets we can trade raw materials (gold, oil, coffee, etc.). Likewise, there are numbers and packages of shares that some companies offer to the public with the intention of capitalizing, such as (Apple, Microsoft, Meta, etc.) and there are even more complex products such as derivative products such as CFDs, futures, binary options among others.

In this book we will focus on the currency market or FOREX, which is nothing other than the negotiation that is carried out with the crossings or interactions of the price of different currencies or currencies of different countries, and that when one appreciates or another depreciates, You will make a profit depending on whether you buy or sell.

Just as you can make profits you could also generate losses since the forex market is the most volatile in the world, which means that it is always moving up and down, and wow! what movements.

Before getting into the matter, it is necessary to point out the main characteristics of the foreign exchange market for the reader's knowledge:

1. The foreign exchange market is the one that moves the largest volume of cash in the world. (Approximately 3 trillion dollars are moved a day and it is carried out by banks, investment funds, economic groups and individuals like you and me.)
2. It is the one that has the greatest volatility or movement per minute up and down than any other market.

3. In this market the main currencies of the world are found (EURO, AMERICAN DOLLAR, CANADIAN DOLLAR, AUSTRALIAN DOLLAR, POUND STERLING, JAPANESE YEN, AMONG OTHERS)
4. It is open 24 hours a day, 365 days a year and depending on the BROKER (The company in charge of offering us the service and the platform to operate, we can invest at any time we want.)
5. The profits obtained can be very good, just as the losses can be high if a method for operating in currencies is not studied and followed.

It is my responsibility to point out that the foreign exchange market can be very risky if you do not have a coherent strategy and good capital management.
Something that I will explain throughout this book.

Dedication.
I dedicate this book to all those people who want to improve themselves every day and who see through currency trading an opportunity to get ahead in their lives. Many successes, dear reader!

Since what concerns the foreign exchange market and its characteristics has been explained; Now I will begin to explain from the fundamental bases, so, if you already know them, you could jump ahead directly to the strategy.

TYPES OF ANALYSIS

To operate in the currency or FOREX markets you have to take into account two types of analysis, _FUNDAMENTAL ANALYSIS AND TECHNICAL ANALYSIS._

FUNDAMENTAL ANALYSIS

It is that analysis that focuses on the news, political, economic and social decisions of the issuing countries of the currency that we are operating.

This analysis is very important to take into account in financial markets in general since they are very sensitive to the events already mentioned above. These events can trigger bullish or bearish movements in our entries, thus putting the operation at risk or, in the best of cases, giving us an unexpected advantage.

For example (in a hypothetical news), if a cut in crude oil supply to the United States by Saudi Arabia is announced, this news would cause the US DOLLAR to depreciate and fall in value by several points, and yes, we are in an operation where we decide to buy the dollar, then this would make us lose our capital in this operation.

TECHNICAL ANALYSIS

This type of analysis is carried out through graphs and indicators that we will need to operate.
In this concept we have four types of graphics:

LINE CHART

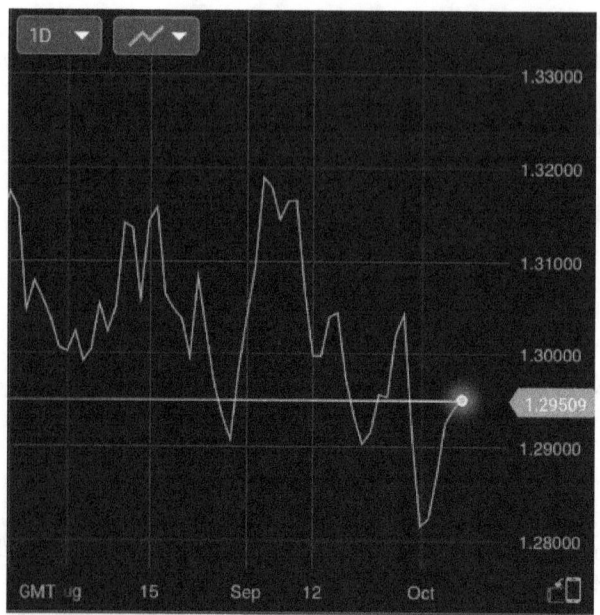

AREA CHART

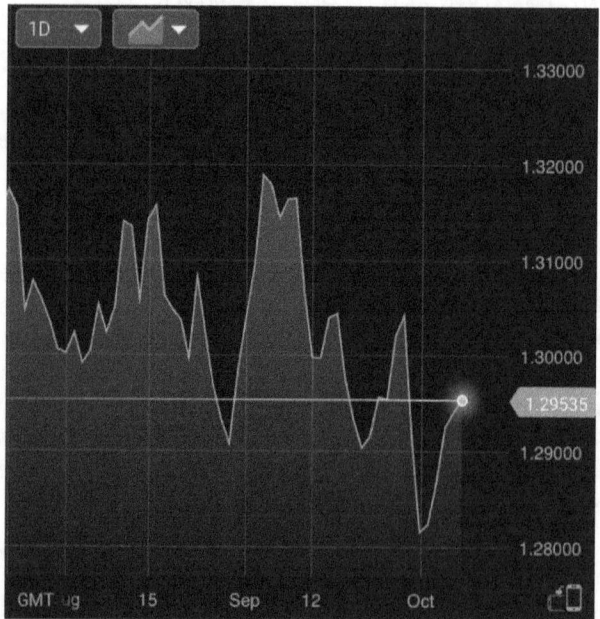

BAR GRAPHIC

JAPANESE CANDLE CHART

I have left the Japanese candlestick chart larger on purpose since it is necessary for you to observe it very well because it will be the type of chart that we will use for the analysis, without detracting from the other types of charts, the truth is that the strategy It is most effective with Japanese candlesticks, and that is why it is the most used type of chart.

Even so, the other types of charts can be used for a more general view of what is happening with the currency cross we select.

JAPANESE CANDLES

Japanese candlesticks are a charting and analysis technique used in economics initially by the Japanese. They emerged in Japan in the 18th century, in the rice market to analyze it more accurately.

It is currently the type of chart most used by TRADERS around the world (people or representatives of institutions that trade or operate in financial markets). Since at the time of technical analysis, Japanese candles reflect the history of the candle, when it finishes forming or the position where it is born or withers. Knowing the history of the candle will help us analyze the history of the price in a certain period of time.

Here we have them.

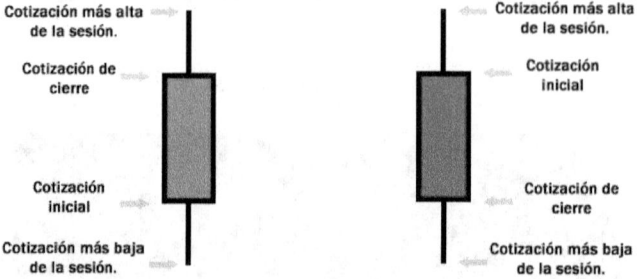

The initial quote is the value or price of the currency at the beginning of the candle or when it is born.

The closing quote is the value or price of the currency in which the candle ended its life.

Lowest price of the session, it is the lowest price the candle has ever reached in its lifetime.

Highest quote of the session, it is the highest price the candle has ever reached in its lifetime.

Japanese candles do not always have these shapes, in fact, they have various shapes and sizes that I will explain later, however, it is necessary to explain that each **session** depends on the type of temporality or time period in which the candle was formed.

CANDLE CHART TEMPORALITIES

In the Japanese candlestick chart and in the other types of charts that I mentioned above, different temporalities can be analyzed and for each time period the chart will be different, this is important to understand since it will help us for the strategy.

Below I will show examples. (All charts are of the same currency cross USD/CAD, but with different timings)

1 DAY CHART

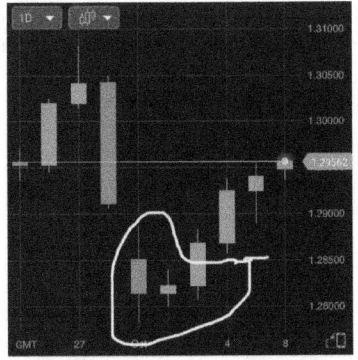

I have marked this candle within a cord because it will be the one we will analyze, note that in the upper left corner is the 1D temporality is one day. It means that each candle has formed in 1 day, in this case what happens in the cord has formed in approximately 2 and a half days.

4 HOUR CHART

It is very important to understand that what is inside the cord is what happened within the three previous candles on the 1-day chart, since this time frame is 4 hours and therefore each candle that is within this cord has had a life of 4 hours, and after it has formed the next one. Note that it is the same currency but with each temporality its internal structure changes.

1 HOUR CHART

In this time frame we can see many more candles and the chart a little more horizontal, this is because that is what is inside the 4-hour and 1-day candles. Here in this chart, each candle we observed had a lifetime of 1 hour, that is, in one hour it was formed and then in another hour the next candle was born.

15 MINUTE CHART

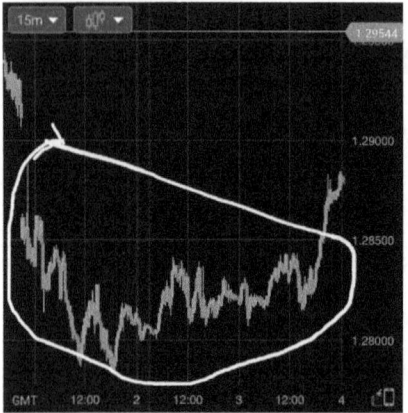

This is a much smaller chart, in fact, I had to zoom out so that the shape of the chart can be distinguished, since if I zoomed in it would not be understood, here each of the candles is almost not visible, only one can be distinguished. trend similar to the previous ones, this is what happens within the candles of the 1 hour, 4 hour, 1 day chart candles.

5 MINUTE CHART

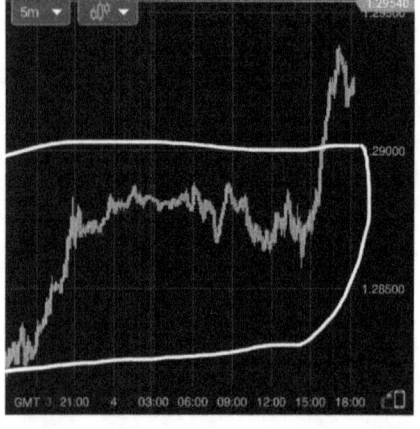

Here you can only distinguish the final part of the trend since the zoom does not allow you to zoom out any further, this is one of the lowest levels of temporalities and reflects what happens within the times previously explained.

CONCLUSION

The longer the time frame of the chart, the more candles can be found in shorter time frames, and therefore the many trends that have formed.

This means that as the temporality increases, the number of candles within it also increases. It is as if within a great mountain we find many large stones and, in turn, within these same stones many small stones.

Please take the time to understand this concept as it is important to the strategy on which this book is based.

TYPES OF JAPANESE CANDLES

At this point in the book, thanks to the previous charts you will surely have noticed that the candles are not the same and that some take different shapes and colors.
This is due to the price action at the present moment. But, above all, to the battle between supply and demand along with news, political decisions and other factors that I will explain later. Everything is discounted in the price, or, in other words, all information available to investors is included in the price.

Returning to the topic, there are several types of Japanese candles and some with similar physical characteristics. These have been grouped under different names to be described.

For the time it would take us to explain all of them we will base ourselves on the most important ones, in fact, rather than the names it is better to understand the direction they have decided to take and why they have taken their form. Thanks to this, we will understand the behavior of the candles and what they represent, or what they want to tell us on the chart.

The main ones are:

BULLISH CANDLES: These are those that are born at a minimum and close at a maximum. They are generally green or white in color and what they indicate to us is that the direction of the price is moving upward.

BEARISH CANDLES: They are those that are born at a maximum and close at a minimum. They are generally red or black and what they indicate to us is that the direction of the price is moving downwards.

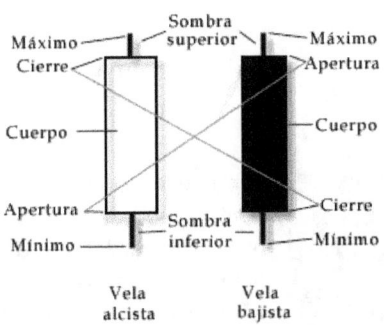

Now, I will present other types of candles that tend to be the most common on charts and by finding them, we can take safer buy or sell positions.

BEARISH ENVELOPE CANDLE:

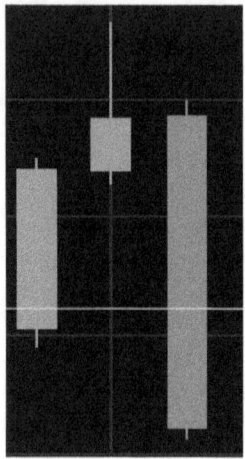

It is the red candle shown on the chart, this candle indicates a downward trend change as it completely envelops the other two previous bullish green candles, usually we find this candle at the highest part of an uptrend.

When we observe this candle it would be very convenient to trade sell or short.

BULLISH ENVELOPE CANDLE:

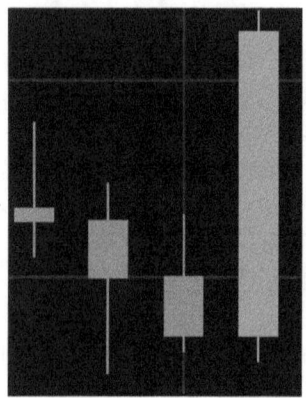

Here we can see an engulfing candle like the previous one, only this one is bullish. Note how it easily envelops the other three bearish candles, this indicates a change in trend upwards, it would be advisable to enter a buy if we see this opportunity.

Generally this type of candle is found at the end of a downtrend.

HANGED MAN:

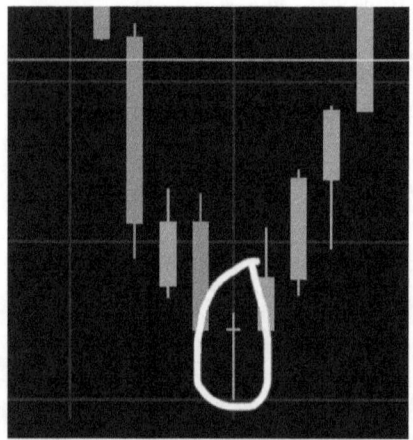

This type of candle indicates a change in upward or bullish trend, since they are usually found at the end of a downward trend, their reliability is very high, their figure is similar to that of a hanging man and this is It is because the price tried to go down further, but the strength of the market pushed it back until it formed a new upward trend.

INVERTED HAMMER OR SHOOTING STAR:

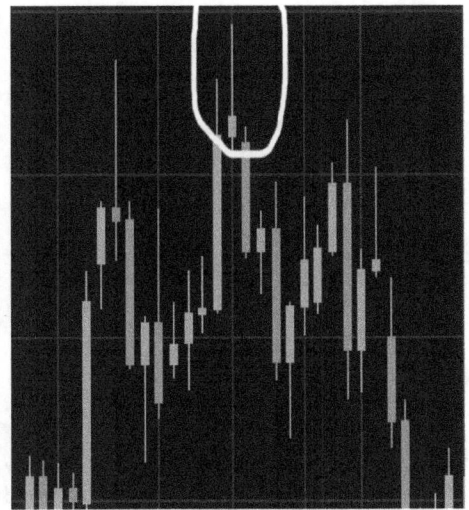

This type of candle is the opposite of the hanging man, and represents a downward or bearish trend change. It usually appears at the end of an uptrend and its reliability is very high.

The concept is exactly the same, since in this case the price should have risen more, however the force of the market pushed it down, thus forming the shooting star. Note that a bearish trend is born after this candle.

DOJIS CANDLES:

These types of candles are very important to take into account since they show us indecision in the market. It means that buyers and sellers have very similar strength and the price cannot decide where it wants to go.

It is important, therefore, not to enter the market when these types of candles appear since we do not really know where the price will go, as the chart shows. At first there is indecision, then the price takes an upward direction on the large green candle, and then regrets it and retreats on the next red candle.

It is better to wait for the price to decide to take a direction and then choose to enter.

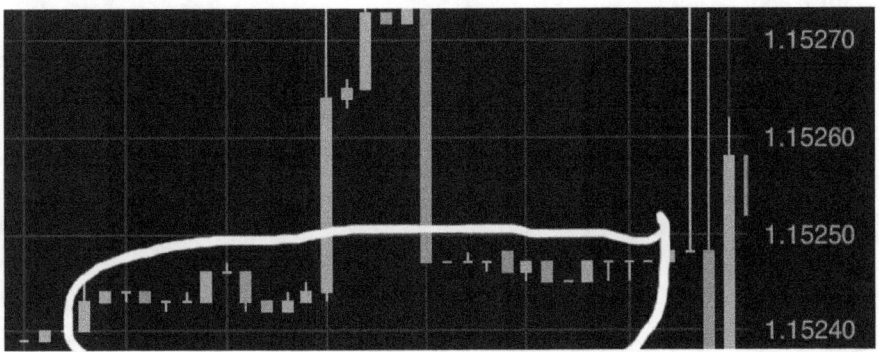

TYPES OF TREND

Welcome to the world of trends, that is, to the interpretation of market forces

The golden rule is: ***"ALWAYS TRADE IN THE DIRECTION OF THE TREND, NEVER AGAINST IT".***

A trend that forms in FOREX is the direction that the price of the asset decides to take when it is influenced by market forces.

TREND LINE

The trend line is an indicator that is used to determine a trend within the graph. We draw it by joining 2 or more points at the maximum or minimum prices depending on the type of trend we find.

It is important to take into account that the trend line serves to determine the direction of the price, and at what point it is likely to bounce up or down. It is also used to determine a change in trend direction when the line is broken.

*REINFORCEMENT CONCEPT

THE STRENGTH OF THE MARKET

It is the strength that market participants have, I mean buyers and sellers.

TYPES OF TREND

-Upward Trend:

Greater number of buyers or greater number of purchase operations. We speak of an uptrend when we take 2 or more candles at their lows and join them with a straight line. Only then does it become a trend.

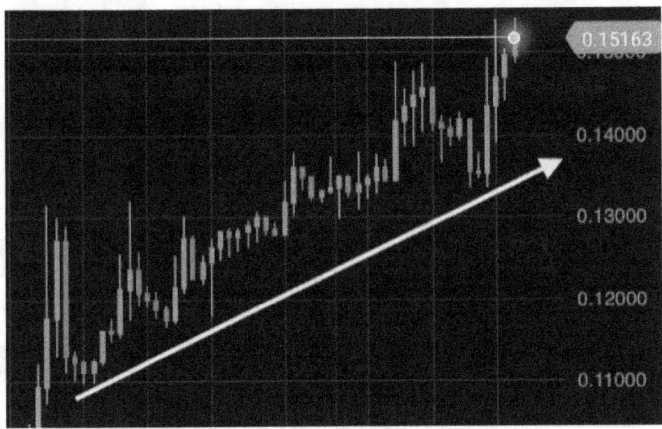

-Downward trend:

Greater number of sellers in the market or greater number of sales orders. We speak of a bearish trend when we take 2 or more candles at their highs and join them with a straight line. Only then does it become a trend.

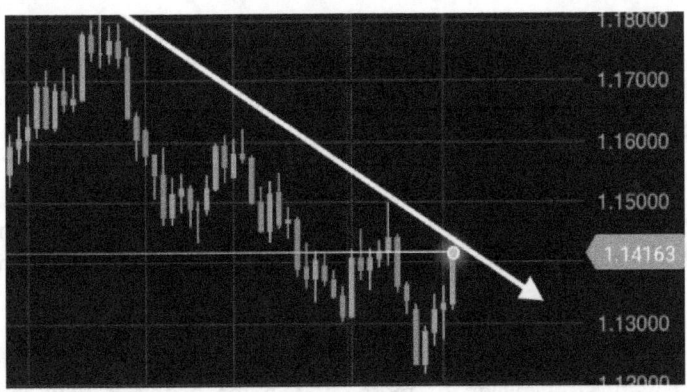

-Side:

Balance between buying and selling forces (supply and demand), and consequently a market direction is not decided. It is represented by drawing maximums and minimums of two or more points of both trends to graph it.

I do not recommend trading them, since obviously the final direction is unknown and there is a lot of uncertainty. In this case, it is better to wait for the market to decide to enter a safer position. However, lateral operations can be performed. And if you find a good opportunity, you could trade in the short term depending on the timing of the chart you choose. Even so, I recommend having a lot of control over the operation at all times since false breakouts often appear on the sides.

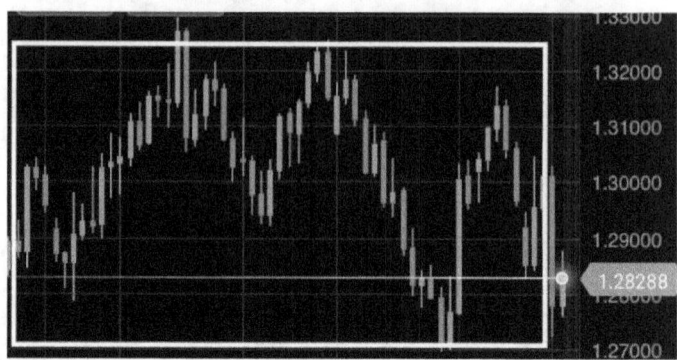

Example of trend interpretation:

Suppose that in the EUR/USD market there are more buyers than sellers, this will then cause the trend to be bullish and will remain in that direction until the amount of sales is greater or more sellers enter the market which will cause a drop in the price. and therefore a change in trend to bearish.

WHAT HAPPENS WHEN AN INVESTMENT FUND OR A BIG BANK ENTERS THE GAME?

Investment funds and banks are places where people place their money to receive benefits on their savings. Therefore, they are investment institutions with high monetary capital. Furthermore, they also invest in the financial markets just like you and I.

The difference is that when these institutions open an operation, they do so with millions and millions of dollars. Which often causes the market to change direction in its favor.

As you will understand, entering with $5,000 dollars with an order is not the same as entering with $200 million or more. And in reality this is how the large market participants are the ones that generally move the price. As small investors, the only thing we can do is operate with them in their favor and in the direction of the market.

THE IMPORTANCE OF THE NEWS

As I explained previously, the currency market is very sensitive to political, economic and social decisions that may affect the countries where its currency is quoted.

However, in general these decisions do not generate a great change in high temporalities. Generally, once this news passes, the direction of the market continues its previous course, as can be seen in the following graphic example:

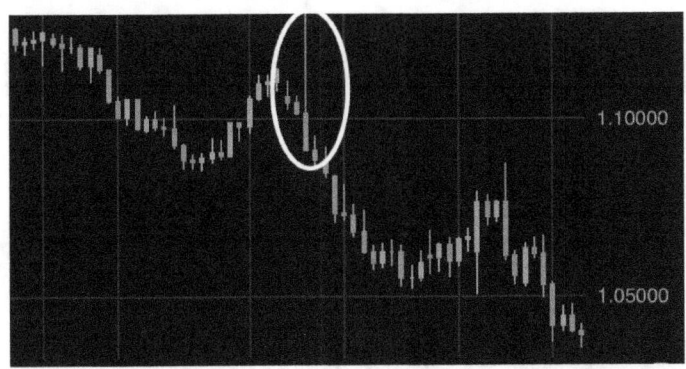

Can we size the great wick that formed?

Well, surely at the time it was a large green candle created by some strong news since the chart is for 1 day. Which means that he traveled a long way and many points, this in turn means that if someone at that precise moment had an open operation with a bearish direction they would have lost it. However, at the end of the event the candle returned to its original position to continue the trend.

But it's not always like this.

In the previous example, the candle was triggered on a 1-day chart, which means that the news was very strong or had a great impact, and that, at the end of the news, the candle returned to its original position to continue with the main trend.

But sometimes the news becomes so strong or momentous that it changes the direction of the market and it no longer recovers in the original direction.

For this reason it is important to protect ourselves against the negative volatility that may exist in the market, and we will achieve this thanks to our strategy, and the STOPS LOSS that I will explain later.

TEMPORALITIES.
(MAIN, SECONDARY AND THIRD TREND)

Within the trend types (bullish, bearish and sideways), as well as in the candlestick chart, these change according to their temporality and not all of them have the same market strength. So not all trends have the same importance to take into account.

Everything will depend on our strategy when operating.

MAIN TREND

It is the strongest of all, since it has been developing for longer than the others, therefore it is the one that we have to take into account when applying the strategy. It can be found in charts with high time frames such as 1 day or 1 month at most. Its duration is usually from 3 months to 6 months or more.

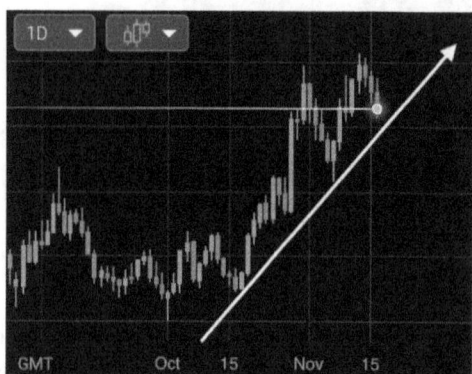

Analyzing this 1-day chart we are talking about a <u>main bullish trend</u> that has formed from the beginning of October to mid-November.

As you can see, the trend line is very accurate to the points so, if the trend line stays straight we will be able to predict at which point the price will likely rise again.

What is shown in the graph is that the buyers have won the price battle and therefore the sellers will have to wait for the price to weaken and take advantage of the opportunity to enter strongly and try to change the direction of the trend in their favor. .

In this case, the red candle is about to touch the trend line which means that, if the pattern remains normal, it would be expected that touching the line we have drawn will cause the price to rise.

SECONDARY TREND

It is the trend that is within the main trend.

When it is in the direction of the main trend, it shows the strength of the market and when it goes against it, it usually shows profit-taking by investors or speculators.

This trend can be found in weekly and daily charts.

In the same graph we can see how the secondary trend is bearish and tries to make the price definitively give up on several occasions, without achieving success. Because the main trend is the strongest.

The secondary trend can last until the main trend ends. That is, after several months or even years. And the candles that form in it can be three days or a week as we see in the chart that, as I explained before, each candle represents 1 day.

THIRD TREND

This is the trend that is within the secondary trend, and like the previous one, it is rebellious to its predecessor, always following the direction of the main trend. It can be observed in much lower time frames of 4 hours, 1 hour or less and its volatility is much higher because the temporality is shorter. This trend can usually last a maximum of 1 day.

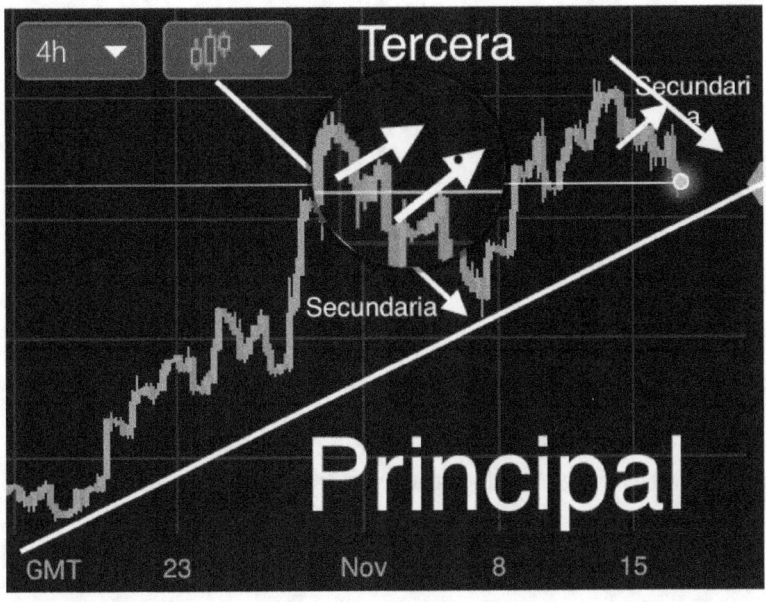

This is the same graph as the two previous examples, note that within the secondary trend several price retracements appear, thus forming the third trend.

SUPPORTS AND RESISTANCES

Now that you know and understand what a trend is, it is time to learn to interpret and even be able to predict what its future will be based on its supports and resistances.

As I explained previously, a trend is the direction that the price takes in technical analysis. However, these are not perpetual in time, but change direction or may end as they approach their supports and resistances.

A support:

It is a minimum limit where the price stops to bounce towards an upward direction, this is drawn by joining 3, 4 or more minimum points on the chart you are analyzing. (Supports are the price floor)

A resistor:

It is a maximum limit where the price stops to bounce towards a bearish direction, this is drawn by joining 3, 4 or more maximum points on the chart you are analyzing. (Resistances are the price ceiling)

In reality, you could say that supports and resistances are historical points on the chart at which the price has once stopped and is likely to do so again in the future.

If, when analyzing, you can see that a trend is about to end, because it is approaching support or resistance, you will have a great advantage when trading.

Does that mean then that the supports and resistances are 100% safe?

No, since as in everything there is another possibility, imagine that the price is close to a support or resistance, and it manages to break it, what happens then?

Two things can happen:

1. Let the candle pierce the support or resistance a little, and after a certain time it returns to the limits to bounce like a ball in the opposite direction. If this happens, the support or resistance will have fulfilled its function.

2. May the candle with great force pierce the support or resistance, and it continue its direction without changing its course. This example is very common, and is a great indicator that the market has decided to take a new stable direction in the long term

(depending on the time frame in which it is operating). If this happens, it is likely that a new trend has been born.

*REINFORCEMENT INFORMATION

Let's remember the previous chapter on trends; We talked about the sides and we said that they are formed by price indecision. It is on the sides where we always find support and resistance, and, in fact, it is important to understand that bullish and bearish trends are always made up of sides.

SIDE TEMPORALITIES

The sides, as well as the candles, have a lifespan (so to speak) and their duration will depend on the temporality of the chart being analyzed.

For example, on one side of a 1 minute chart, you will be able to see changes such as breaks of supports and resistances in perhaps 5 or 10 minutes, so this side will not last long. However, if we analyze a side formed on a 1 year chart, we will possibly have to wait 2 or 3 years to see the changes and it is completely normal due to the time in which each candle forms.

TECHNICAL INDICATORS

This book will not go into depth about indicators, but I will explain the topic.

Indicators are a very useful tool in technical analysis; they help us look for the best entries and at the same time confirm the direction of the trend.

In the world of indicators there is a great variety, however, the best and most used are the following:

RSI (*Relative Strength Index*)

The RSI is an oscillator-type indicator that reflects the relative strength of bullish movements, compared to bearish movements. It is used as the best indicator by traders to measure the strength of a trend and identify trend end signals.

In order to interpret this index, it is basically necessary to analyze levels 70 and 30. When the price is at levels greater than or equal to 70, it means that the asset is overbought and when it is at levels equal to or less than 30, it means, at the same time, On the contrary, it is oversold. Which in turn means that if we are in Buy and the price in the RSI is at level 70 or more, it will be best to close the operation and look for sales and, on the contrary, if it is in Sell, since in both cases the price is very likely to turn around when it is at those levels.

To configure the SRI, it is recommended to leave it by default at the last 14 movements.

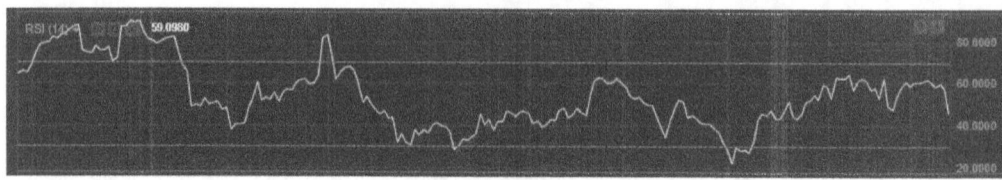

Simple moving averages

A simple moving average is the arithmetic average of the previous data, in short, it would be a line that averages the movements of an asset, whether it is the last periods you choose, for example, we have moving averages of 50 last movements or of 100 or of 200, in short, you can choose the one you want according to your operation.

And why are moving averages so important?

Because basically because they act as supports and resistances, stopping the price or breaking strongly. The most used moving averages are the 50, 100 and 200 period, where the latter is considered almost an impenetrable support or resistance, since the wider the moving average, the stronger it becomes to be overcome, and when this happens the price skyrockets, although most of the time it is a difficult task.

As can be seen in this graph, the price sometimes bounces with the 50-movement average without being able to break it, however, when it finally does so, it does so with force that is expressed with a large red candle, where it goes down to finally be stopped. by the average of 200 periods.

One moving average strategy is to buy when the smaller average crosses the larger average in a bullish direction and sell when the smaller average crosses the larger average in a bearish direction.

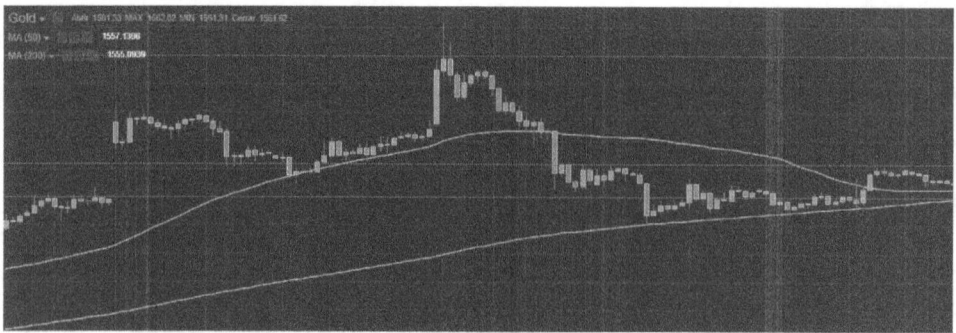

MACD

The MACD is an indicator used in technical analysis both to detect trends and trend changes and to know if the price of an asset is overbought or oversold. This indicator tells the difference between a fast (short period) exponential moving average (EMA) and a slow (longer period) EMA.

To interpret the MACD it is important to analyze 3 possible scenarios:

1. The crossing of their averages: When these cross in a bullish direction it is a buy signal and when they cross in a bearish direction, a sell signal.

2. When the Zero Line is crossed: When both averages cross the middle line, also called the zero line, it should be taken as a buy or sell signal depending on the direction of the crossing. In short, if it crosses the zero line upwards, it is a sign of buy and if it goes down it is a sale.

Now let's analyze the following graph:

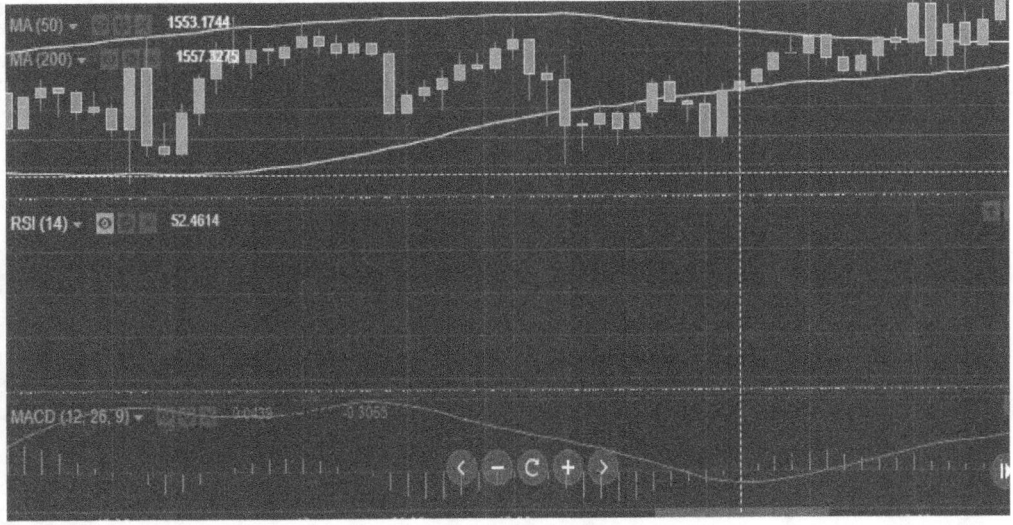

Right where the cursor is, you can see how as soon as the MACD lines cross upwards, the price begins to rise and when it crosses the zero line the price continues the trend.

Now let's analyze the graph with the three indicators explained above:

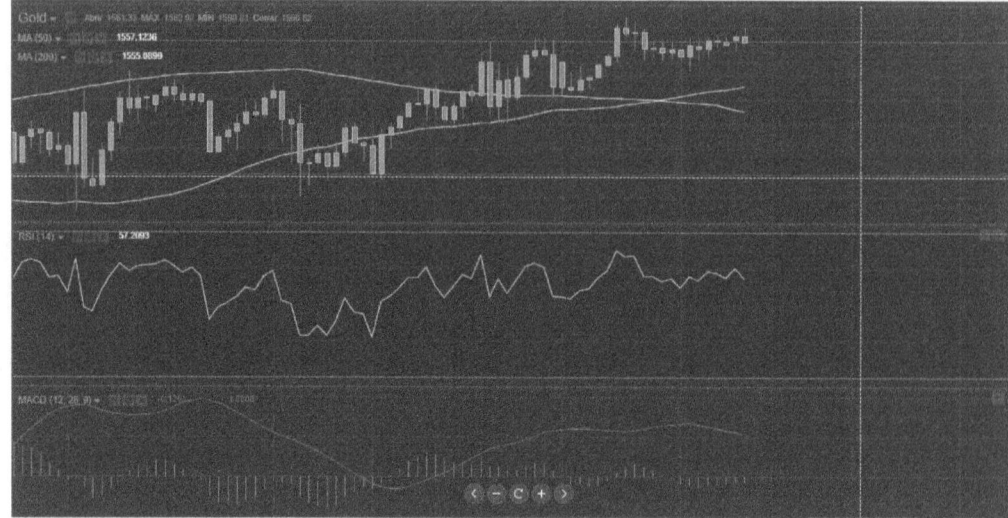

As can be seen in the graph at the beginning, the moving averages of 50 and 200 come into effect, initially the 50 is pierced and then bounces against the 200 and follows the main trend, which is bullish.

According to what the RSI indicates, it is not yet at oversold levels, so we can still continue buying.

And the MACD showed us the bullish momentum at the time of the crossing of the averages.

However, as the price develops, according to the subsequent analysis it seems that the price is about to turn around since the MACD is already crossed downwards and so are the moving averages, which would be enough indication to close positions. bullish and try to enter purchases.

THE STRATEGY

Well, at this point we will begin with the strategy, it is important to emphasize that it must be followed to the letter for it to work, since it has been carefully analyzed and tested many times.

To describe the strategy I have developed, it is basically summarized in this sentence. "You have to minimize losses and let profits run"

Do we expect losses?
The answer is of course yes.

In the currency market nothing is said and no matter how much you learn strategies of all kinds, losses will always exist. However, if we control losses so that they are minimal and uncontrollable profits so to speak, the strategy will be successful.

COMPONENTS OF THE STRATEGY

MONETARY MANAGEMENT

It is the correct management of the cash that you will use to operate.

Many brokers offer platforms where you can start trading with 10 dollars, however, this is the riskiest thing that exists, since, even if the strategy is applied with that minimum amount, the results will not be satisfactory and therefore it will most likely be that the cash is completely lost simply because of the desperation to win.
The indicated amount to operate would be $2,000 dollars since the more money you use, the lower the risk will be, because the multiplier will be lower.

THE MULTIPLIER (LEVERAGE)

All platforms offer them, and it is nothing more than the way to leverage our money, for example:

If you invest $2,000.00 with a multiplier of x 20, it will be equal to investing 40,000.00 real dollars.

It is very simple to calculate the leverage, and according to this same example: if you invested that amount of cash, your profit would be greater than if you invested $2,000.00 with a multiplier of x 5 that gives us 10,000.00 dollars.

However, just as the multiplier can help you win more, it can also make you lose more money, which is why it is important to always maintain a balance between the profit we expect and the losses we expect.

For the strategy I advise using the following table:

VALUE TO INVEST	MULTIPLIER
2000	10
3000	10
4000	9.5
5000	8

In reality, I would advise using a maximum multiplier of 10 with any amount of cash, there is no problem, however, I also advise that the more cash you have, it is preferable to lower the multiplier; But I emphasize that it is not more than 10 since it would be very risky for your capital.

RULES TO OPERATE

- The strategy says not to operate more than 3 times a day and always do it during times of high volatility or in the morning or afternoon, since this way you will be able to realize in which direction the price is heading depending on the type of trend you are taking.

- Do not operate at night or during low volatility hours, since it is difficult to try to predict the price movement because the candles move more slowly.

- It also says that you should not operate on holidays, when strong news appears, nor during market opening or closing hours since there is a lot of uncertainty.

- Operations cannot be left open on market closing days (weekend days).

The idea is that if you operate a maximum of 3 times a day you can lose 1 operation and win the other 2 or in the best case win all 3 consecutively.

If you lose more than 2 times, you can choose to leave the operations there for that day and rethink what happened and try again with more strength and with a cool head the next day, I repeat, it is normal to lose and it will surely happen to you too.

Benefits: Your profit will be a minimum of 1% of the capital invested per day, for example, if you invest $2,000.00, then your profit will be 20 dollars. The strategy works as long as you earn at least that net amount per day, subtracting losses of course. That way in 22 business days, you will have earned $440.

Losses: Losses are calculated at a maximum of 1% daily. Following the same previous example as the profit, the loss will be a maximum of 20 dollars on the day.

In this way, if you operate 3 times, the monetary strategy is that you win on two occasions and may lose on one, or at least reach one winning opportunity per day. This way it can be profitable in the long term.

APPLYING THE STRATEGY TO THE OPERATION

Discounting the information about the components of the strategy and the rules to operate, we will move on to the operation itself.

Step 1. Analyze the economic calendar.

- Let's say you want to trade today in the JPY/USD market, then the first thing you should do is analyze the economic calendar. For this, I suggest the INVESTING.COM page.

    I have no sponsorship from Investing.com, but in my opinion it is a very useful and zero-cost site.

```
18:50  JPY    Encuesta Tankan: grandes
▼▼▼   🇯🇵    empresas manufactureras (1T)
              Actual: 11 | Prev.: 10 | Anterior: 13 ♦

18:50  JPY    Encuesta Tankan: grandes
▼▼▼   🇯🇵    empresas no manufactureras
              (1T)
              Actual: 34 | Prev.: 33 | Anterior: 32 ♦

18:50  JPY    Encuesta Tankan: previsiones de
▼▼▼   🇯🇵    la gran industria manufacturera
              (1T)
              Actual: 10 | Prev.: 11 | Anterior: 8

18:50  JPY    Encuesta Tankan: Capex en la
▼▼▼   🇯🇵    gran industria (1T)
              Actual: 4,0% | Prev.: 9,2% |
              Anterior: 13,2% ♦

18:50  JPY    Encuesta Tankan: Capex en la
▼▼▼   🇯🇵    pequeña industria (1T)
              Actual: -3,6% | Prev.: | Anterior: 8,3% ♦
```

Within the economic calendar, there are the figures of a "bull" on each piece of news. This symbolizes the degree of volatility that the news is expected to generate within the market, since it is important news.

If the news has 3 bulls, <u>you should not enter the market at that time.</u> For my part, I would recommend up to 2 bulls.

Step 2. Analyze the graph.

This step is essential since a bad entry will cause the strategy to not work and losses will occur. So, to mitigate this risk it will be necessary to analyze the graph of the asset we are going to operate on at least 15 minutes before the operation. Regardless of the asset that is going to be operated, I suggest doing it between the hours of 10:00 am and 1:00 pm American time. Since, at this time first, by not knowing the direction of the price at the opening, there is a lot of risk when entering as soon as the market opens.

It is best to wait 30 minutes or 1 hour until the market defines the direction of the trend for that day. On the other hand, I recommend trading until before closing and more specifically until 1 pm, since most of the daily volume moves during that time.

When entering the chart, the first thing we will do is analyze the dominant trend through technical analysis (support and resistance lines) and technical indicators. Once the dominant trend is identified on the 1-hour chart, we will look for an up or down entry on the 1-5 minute chart. Preferably, I suggest looking for a correlation between the 1 hour and 5 minute charts, in order to take a position on the 1 minute chart.

Step 3. Find the best possible entry.

IN UPWARD TREND:

The entry will always be executed on a bearish retracement. For example, if the 1-hour chart identifies that we are in an uptrend but that at the moment we are in a retracement that will allow the trend to continue, and that the upward rebound is already taking place from the support line, then we will look for the best entry on the 1 or 5 min chart.

As well as the case detailed below:

CHART IN 1 HOUR

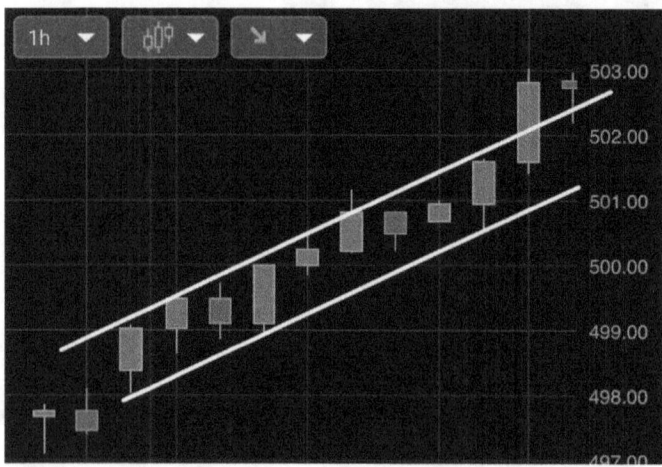

CHART IN 5 MINUTES

GRAPH IN 1 MINUTE (THE ENTRANCE)

I apologize in advance as I couldn't find the 1 min graph. However, the point of the entry can be illustrated in the same 5 min chart.

In this case, we are entering right after the bearish retracement once the price has stabilized at the support line and surpassed the previous candle.

This example can perfectly illustrate the importance of leverage control, since it is not possible to accurately detect which candle will continue the bullish movement, and therefore, on three occasions the price touched the support line. To avoid risk, it is important not to enter with a very high leverage so that the price has the freedom to move even against us, until the trend resumes.

Once the price resumes the trend, the profit-taking objective will depend on the medium-term horizon (1 to 4 hours).

STOP LOSS: The stop loss must be located below the trend line.

As the price advances upwards, the stop loss must be adjusted upwards until we are in a position in which the risk has been mitigated and we are almost guaranteed profits.

IN DOWNWARD AND SIDEWARD TREND:

Exactly the same way of operating applies. However, I do not recommend operating on the sides as much as they are generally rest areas in the price where a trend is usually resumed later or there may be a change in trend. In both cases, it is usually unpredictable. And this is where we will rely on technical indicators to make a decision.

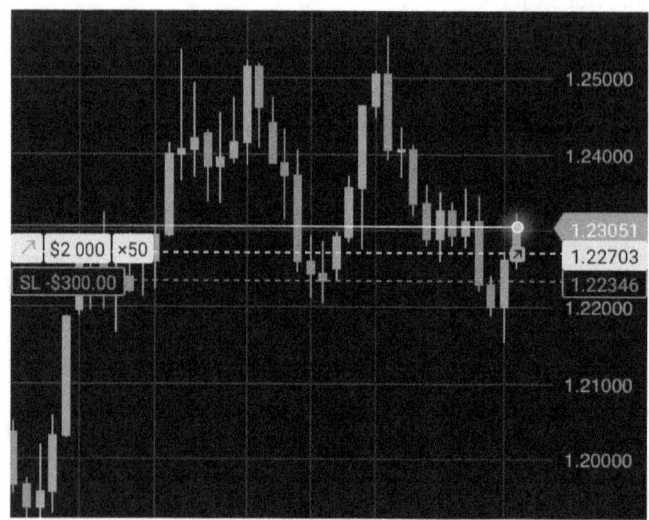

In the case of operating in a bearish trend, we will look for an upward retracement as in the following image:

WHAT TO DO IF WE HAVE DOUBTS ABOUT THE ENTRY OR REGARDING THE TREND?

In this case, it is advisable to rely mainly on technical indicators such as the RSI. Although it will always be better to avoid this entry and wait for another opportunity.

PERSONAL RECOMMENDATION :

My recommendation will always be to look for a life opportunity through trading, what do I mean by this? That there is sufficient preparation, both on the monetary side and on the strategy side, to not look for many entries, but rather to look for an entry that can change our lives and keep it open for the medium and long term until the risk has been 100% covered. and the only thing we obtain from then on is profits. This at the end of the day will depend on the following factors:

-Moderate or low leverage.
-A good entry.
-Medium and long-term horizon for taking benefits.

In this way, I encourage you, dear reader, to plan ahead and apply this strategy without pressure.

Remember that the more cash and less leverage used, the lower the risk of losing money; and, if we add to that a good entry, your chances of success will be greater. And in my point of view, that is the best way to operate.

www.ingramcontent.com/pod-product-compliance
Lightning Source LLC
Chambersburg PA
CBHW071000220526
45471CB00007B/3116